Discerning God's Active Involvement in Your Life

Discerning God's Active Involvement in Your Life

What Is God Up To Now?

Frederick Castor

Copyright © 2016 Frederick Castor
Fort Collins, Colorado

ISBN-13: 978-1530757893
ISBN-10: 1530757894
CreateSpace Independent Publishing Platform

All rights reserved.

Cover photo by Greg Halac
Author photo by John Eisele

Cover design by Steve Hays
www.fort-collins-graphic-design.com

Interior layout and design by Jennifer Top
www.jennifertop.com

To my family

Contents

Acknowledgments .... *ix*
Launching the Exploration 1
Miracles—God's Mysterious Ways 7
The Critical Crossover 11
Transitioning from Belief through Doubt into Faith 15
Faith—God's Pivotal Intrusion into Our Lives 23
Subtle Transformation 27
The Urge to Make a Difference 31
Learning to Live in Two Worlds 35
Inspiration—God's Breath of Life 39
The Magic of Silence 43
Worship—A Hint of Heaven 47
Brainstorming with God 53
Coffee with God 57
Walking and Talking with God 61
Hope—The Sign of God's Activity 65
Faith versus Fear 69
Experiencing Joy and Pain 73
The Heavens Declare the Glory of God 77
Nature—God's Work of Art 81
Music—Effervescence from God's Soul 85

Making Better Choices 89
Forgiveness—Healing 95
Healing of the Mind 101
God's Uncanny Timing 105
Transcending Excessive Stress 109
Transcending Temptation 115
Struggling with Depression 121
Conclusion 127
About the Cover *131*

Acknowledgments

I wish to acknowledge and thank the following people for their assistance and support: Robin Castor, Wanda Knauer, Richard Bansemer, Jane Nicolet, Steve Hays, Jennifer Top, Linda Bobbitt and Dorothy Zelenko for sharing their unique gifts that have made this endeavor possible.

Jane O'Leary, Claire Gilliland, Jeremy and Jenn Castor, Don Imsland, Douglas Anderson, Karen Barber, Chris Bachman and Rob Arone for their support throughout this process. Your timing has been right on!

The Father in Heaven for assigning me this task in the middle of the night. The Holy Spirit for flooding my mind with thoughts and words faster than I could write, and for making readers aware of God's uncanny involvement in their lives.

Launching the Exploration

One of the most incredible surprises we can ever experience is *discovering God's involvement in our lives*. Nothing in all of life is more deeply satisfying than learning the extent of this divine activity. Our relationship with God can be truly magnanimous as well as curiously mysterious.

Oneness with God indubitably is the apex of all human experience. It is the virtual heaven on earth. Graciously, it is open to anyone who seeks to perceive the big picture of God's magnificent plan, rather than being totally locked into one's own daily concerns. Spiritual development is growing beyond one's self-centered interests into an expanded world view—God's view.

You may consider your connection with God as the most important thing in your life, or you may consider it to be a matter of only mild interest. Its significance to you may move back and forth along a continuum from day to day. However, the very fact that you are even reading this denotes awareness on your part that there is something inside you that recognizes being related to God on some level holds at least a modicum of interest. Raising the level of that relationship can be a highly productive investment. *Discerning God's active involvement in your life* and nurturing that involvement are most worthy of your pursuit because of the enormous, positive impact it can have on your life. This is not a mere religious endeavor, but rather a unique spiritual quest and the whole purpose of this writing.

At the outset it is important to challenge the often held position that God is not disposed toward maintaining personal relationships with us, but remains aloof from such encounters. This view holds that God is more of a universal power rather than a personal deity. It can be difficult for a person with this perspective to move beyond it, in order to experience a more personal God. Although, whenever such a breakthrough does occur, it can be tremendously rewarding and personally exciting.

Effective communication is paramount for developing and maintaining a healthy relationship with anyone. It is no different with God. Unfortunately, for many people the idea of God's actually communicating with them is a totally alien idea. Their bewilderment, and even rejection of the idea, is understandable since it probably has not been any part of their experience. On the other hand, for the many people who have been blessed by experiencing and recognizing God's messages to them, communication with the Holy One has become an accepted part of their daily lives. History is overflowing with cases of this nature.

A significant part of this communication is *listening*—becoming alert to how God engages us and becomes involved in our lives. We pray (speak) and we listen (meditate). Sometimes merely completing that connection—consciously being present to the Holy One—is all that is necessary for the moment. It sounds so simple, but we know from experience that worthy communication with anyone requires constant attention and effort and calls for commitment. It begins with simply paying attention and acknowledging the presence of another—in this case, God.

A vital factor in this discernment equation is the awareness that we always live in God's presence, although we are inclined not to be cognizant of that reality. We seem to relegate our connection to God to the back burner, perhaps merely to stay warm, but not heated or engaged actively. An essential step in the process of exploring God's place in our lives is the development of a detection system that remains armed at all times, so that whenever and however we receive a signal there is an incoming message from God, we are ready. We need to be alert and allow God to speak to us through whatever medium has been divinely chosen for that moment.

(*Discernment*—recognizing the source of these messages—is the key, and that is a God-gift that comes through grace along with practice and experience.) If God is texting your mind with a message, you can learn to recognize it as being mysteriously connected to God's involvement in your life. It may be hidden in words of a song or a statement in a book or magazine. What you are hearing in your mind, hearing from others, or what you are witnessing might be a message from God, although it is couched in the most casual conversation or ordinary event. Being alert to these endless possibilities should become a guiding principle for daily living. It is a new way to listen and imperative for *discernment*.

While pursuing this exploration new experiences begin to occur. Life expands. You begin to realize that in your past you have most likely downsized your perception of God's world to the size of your own personal interest and experience, but now become increasingly awed by how expansive God's created order actually is. Mysteriously you become aware that there is also an awesome spiritual world, paralleling the physical world, that is just as real and equally as exciting. As you begin to dip into this spiritual world you will encounter God on a different level. A whole new world will open to you, and you will begin sensing that God has been deeply involved in your life all along. As you look back over your life you will be surprised to discover God's handprint in some of the most significant events and turning points that you can recall. They become aha moments. Even if you are new to this experience and perhaps skeptical, but open, I encourage you to give it a test run. It has become an invaluable lifestyle for people of every era, and it promises the same for you.

Following are essays that have been written with a clear awareness of a long and pregnant tradition of spirituality on the one hand, and on the other hand, a cognizance of a sad lack of discernment of this sacred involvement. It is hoped that if you are on the cusp of testing the waters of a more serious spiritual life you will be awakened to its potential, have your ego softened, and be moved to give God's Spirit a chance by granting greater access to your own spirit. Hopefully, this material will help you discern more distinctly God's activity in your life, encourage you to appropriate its eye-opening and far reaching benefits, and finally, motivate you to internalize and utilize its amazing energy and astonishing power.

As you embark upon this exploration pray: Teach me how to listen for your message, O Lord, and give me endless patience as this captivating mystery unfolds within me.

Suggestions: Offer brief prayers before and after each reading. Slowly read no more than one essay in any given day. Reread it, then allow time for your mind and spirit to assimilate the concepts that are presented. Blessed journey!

Note: Because of the nature and format of these essays, they readily lend themselves to group discussions. At the end of each one is a question for further personal thought and possible group discussion. Space is available for recording your responses and notes.

Miracles—God's Mysterious Ways

The technical and theological definition of miracle is the alteration of the natural order. According to this definition a miracle is the enactment of something that does not normally or naturally occur on its own. The scriptures cite many miracles, all of which fit this definition. They are viewed as extraordinary acts of God that change the natural course of events and in turn alter their outcomes.

Furthermore, a miracle always has a specific purpose that is more important than the mystery of the miracles itself. The message is more significant than the script that conveys it. If we experience a miracle of God in our lives, we are constrained not only to celebrate the miracle itself, but especially to search for the message behind it, for some evidence of what God has in mind for us. What is God attempting to say to us through this occurrence? *What is God up to now?*

Perhaps the most common and sought after miracles we might experience are for physical healing for ourselves or someone else for whom we hold concern. While there might be some question about a particular healing being miraculous when medical assistance has been given, the core reality in any healing is that God's creative presence and healing power are involved and are the ultimate cause behind the effect. Every physical healing has a basic spiritual component. The message behind the healing is always about *God's involvement in our lives.* The healing is not an end in itself, but is intended to draw us closer to the Holy One. We should always keep that in focus.

Beyond physical healing there are other areas of our lives where inexplicable events occur. For example: we are led into certain professions or occupations through gifts of ability and talent. A sequence of events may lead us to pursue a particular opportunity that has opened to us. God, indeed, can be and often is involved in what goes on. In these cases discernment of that reality is an added gift.

The part we are called to recognize is that our relationship with God is never static or inactive, but always in gear and functioning. The more we are aware of that fact, and the more open we are to God's activity, the more clear its message becomes to us. Give God an opening into your life and miracles will inevitably occur. Unbelievable things will happen. New dimensions of life will spontaneously appear like new growth on a tree. Life will take on an exquisite flavor never before tasted.

One of God's most impressive miracles is that of making us new creatures—awakening within us a spiritual awareness that is new, curious and promising. There is no more precious experience. This amazing change is so incredible that is can only be attributed to divine power.

Perhaps we overuse the term miracle, but the many wonderful things that occur in our lives do astound us. We cannot explain why they happen, so we call them miracles. How often have events in your life taken mysterious turns? You were spared an accident. You somehow became aware that you should go in a different direction or try something you never thought of doing. These inexplicable directives may not have all the nuances of Biblical miracles, but their awesomeness earns them our choice to use the term *miracle*.

The purpose of this message is not to quibble over the definition of a term, but to recognize God's involvement in our daily lives in mysterious ways. Perhaps that is the most useful definition of miracle—*God's mysterious involvement in our lives*.

Question

Using the definition of miracles as God's mysterious involvement in our lives, what examples of this can you recall in your life?

The Critical Crossover

There are at least two different kinds of shopping in which we might engage. One has typically been labeled window shopping. This is a casual, uncommitted strolling, while observing the display of various merchandise. It is pleasant, safe and inexpensive. It can be started and stopped at will with little effort or consequences.

On the other hand, there is the more serious shopping that requires greater commitment and more focused attention. It becomes more engaging of our time. It has desire as a motivator, and satisfaction as the goal. It is more deliberate and consuming. We are much more involved in this process. There is considerably more at stake with our actual investment, and the end result hopefully is much more gratifying than casual window shopping.

Changing from one mode of shopping to the other is a major switch in our agenda. Window shopping, while relatively undemanding often leads to more serious shopping, which is a *critical crossover*.

This concept of *critical crossover* can also apply to our spiritual journey in life. We might spend years observing the appearance of a spiritual life from a safe, distant stance, and still remain casual observers with no commitment. We might harbor many positive thoughts about its possibilities, and yet remain on the outside, disengaged and apart from its promises and power for our lives. While it appears to offer whole new dimensions to our lives, it remains unexplored, and therefore unfulfilling, even innocuous. For many people that is where everything stops. No growth develops beyond that point.

It requires a *critical crossover* in order for the power of God to be unleashed into our lives. It is a crossover from casual interest and observation to more serious engagement as with shopping. It moves from casual appreciation to more serious investigation. It moves from wondering and wandering, to a higher level of desire and expectation. It moves from happiness and fun to hope and joy which are far more satisfying and fulfilling. If we are going to gain anything of value from our experience with God, it is essential that we make that *critical crossover*.

The commitment to pursue serious spiritual shopping morphs into an acute awareness there is a significant difference between thinking those good ideas that come to our minds are our own personal constructs, versus awakening to the realization those wonderful thoughts and ideas have actually been deposited into our minds by God—and for a specific purpose. It is our task to discern the source of their origin, as we celebrate their presence in our minds. It is in this process that we become more aware of how intimately God is involved in our lives. That discernment has significant transforming power.

Question

How intense is your desire to become more involved with God; are you satisfied with that intensity?

Transitioning from Belief through Doubt into Faith

If you want to discern God is involved in your life, locate where you think you fit on this continuum of

belief   doubt   faith

It should be obvious what the presumed goal is by virtue of the direction of the flow—*faith*.

Most of us Christians begin with *belief*. That is, we are taught by our parents, the church or perhaps we learn through social relationships that certain things are assumed to be true and sacred, and are to be believed. There is a God who created the earth and life. We are a part of that creation. We are further taught that the Father in heaven sent Jesus to die on the cross to save the world, and that he rose from the dead. Through Jesus' death and resurrection we are saved from our sins and will receive eternal life in our own resurrection.

All the above is a part of a traditional and extensive belief system that has been the church's cornucopia of teachings, distributing it as the truth that, if believed, will set us free from the shackles of sin and win for us the gold medal of everlasting life.

Many of us have grown up within this belief system, and have accepted it to be true and accurate. The conventional understanding is that the single requirement for salvation on our part is affirming these teachings. The rest is up to God's grace. For most of our lives we have been soberly fearful of deviating from these explicit teachings, or even allowing ourselves to question their efficacy.

There are many people who continue to hold on to this simple system of beliefs throughout their lives. They find comfort, strength and assurance in these clearly spelled-out teachings. If any doubt encroaches along the way, they dismiss it as being dangerously wrong and sinful, trusting that what they have believed and still believe is irrefutable and perfectly adequate for their salvation. Any crack in that armor would be devastating to them. They hold tenaciously to the set of beliefs they consider to be inextricably tied to their salvation and eternal life. It is their lifeline. It is their childhood religion, and it works for them—for the moment.

What needs to be said about this way of believing is that it is a very simple, perhaps simplistic, sort of belief. It is unexamined and untested by the strains of life and the challenges of reason. It can work well as long as life also remains simple. However, if and when life becomes complicated, traumatic or more sophisticated, then the simple, untested belief system often is not adequate to withstand the pressures. It is not unusual for people who are equipped with nothing more than this simple belief system to give up on it when under duress. The system fails them and is abandoned because it is not sustainable. Along with the abandonment of the system, often is the concomitant abandonment of the church which initially taught them this belief system. Because no upgrade has occurred everything is discarded as useless.

Doubt is born and begins to grow. However, it must be said parenthetically, this same doubt is essential for the transition into a sustainable faith. Without doubt we remain locked into believing that a simple system of beliefs will sustain us through life's sometimes treacherous path. Then it becomes a gamble, not unlike refusing to buy insurance when the hazards are quite apparent.

People move to the *doubting* stage on the continuum, feeling lost, at sea, because they have nothing designed and available to come to their support in their emotional, physical and mental struggles. Their simple belief system has failed them. They give up on God because, to them, it is obvious that God has given up on them, or perhaps there is no God in the first place. To say that Jesus died for our sins does not minister to them in the midst of life's tribulations. It is no wonder they give up on religion. It has unveiled its own impotency. Their doubt grows, challenging them and often causing them to discard one belief after another.

Many people are caught and become transfixed at that spot on the continuum. Doubt becomes their guiding principle. They seem unable to move on to the next stage—*faith*. In fact, some slip into rank disbelief at this juncture.

People who are stuck in doubt are often uneasy in this no man's land, and search for things to comfort them, and provide them with some sense of security. Some find solace in reason and rational thought or the scientific method as a way of confronting life's challenges. For others, alternate dimensions of life attract them and they find satisfaction elsewhere—recreation, career success, achievement, family.

The belief system that they learned early in life is discarded or put on a shelf, because it no longer serves them in their adult life that is now filled with endless stresses and trials. They learn how to make it through life without any religious beliefs, by honing their own skills and, ironically, by utilizing their God given talents. Unfortunately, they often become arrogant, flaunting their talents while hiding their ominous fears that follow them wherever they go.

Vast numbers of people spend the rest of their lives in the throes of doubt, rather than struggling through it to reach the next stage.

There is one more stage on the continuum of life designed into God's apparent plan. It is faith. Faith is totally different from belief. While belief is ascribing credibility to certain prescribed information pertaining to God, without vetting it, faith on the other hand is an intimate, and loving relationship with God. It is not cognitive, but spiritual, personal, experiential and sustaining. It is not a set of facts *about* God, held to be true, but rather an immediate, uncomplicated relationship *with* the Holy One in which there is open communication, hope, joy and a strong sense of God's involvement in one's life. It is not only a promise for the future, but an existential reality which ultimately proves itself to be more supportive and sustaining than any set of beliefs one might have been taught earlier in life. It also transcends any rational attempts to describe God's indescribable nature and modus operandi.

If and when we move into this final segment on the continuum, life becomes Spirit-directed. We then move into the penultimate stage of God's plan for us, and are astounded, but incessantly grateful, to find ourselves beyond belief, beyond doubt, and in a loving relationship with the Holy One who has apparently put us here for a purpose and equipped us for a mission.

With this transition into faith we embark upon our spiritual journey that is quite different from anything we have experienced earlier. Faith does not demand that we believe, with certainty, specific details that we may have been taught. However, to our amazement, at this stage, these same details in question, may now present themselves as a totally different reality than before, and demonstrate their current viability and value in God's scheme of things. They have the potential of being recharged with new meaning.

Faith, being our relationship with God, is the final stage of God's plan for us here and now because it has no end. It extends into heaven itself, and is the beginning of our life with God that is everlasting. Theologians call this realized eschatology. Eschatology, because it describes end events—realized, because it describes that which is already underway. The image it suggests is that of heaven dipping down into the present in all of its exquisiteness. It is even beyond a taste of the feast to come. It is the actual beginning of the feast itself because it is being with God, which is the essence of the heavenly experience. Discerning how to live with God in this new way, within this new world of reality, is clearly a decisive spiritual experience.

Faith is not a requirement that God makes. Rather, it is the gift God gives us when those loving arms of grace enfold us on the penultimate stage of glory. It is the first of several scenes in the final act of God's incredible drama, written explicitly for us. It will be acted out fully if we are desirous and willing to be seriously engaged and intimately involved with the Holy One. Our will is the key that unlocks this process and sets it into motion. Our self discipline is our investment. Surrounding and upholding it all is the empowering inspiration of God's Holy Spirit.

Questions

Reflect on your personal faith journey. What life experiences have affected significant shifts?

How might God have been involved in these experiences?

Faith—God's Pivotal Intrusion into Our Lives

Faith can be God's most generous gift to us—one that exudes such baffling mystery that it escapes our most acute comprehension. Faith is an uttermost mystery.

The word *faith* enjoys one of the highest employment rates of any term used in describing religious life. It is used to label any number of life experiences with God—often incorrectly.

It is misused to describe a quantity of belief in such statements as: "Have more faith" or "I don't have enough faith." In such cases it is erroneously used to describe an amount of purchasing power one has with God. Having more or less faith according to this incorrect usage quantifies one's religious fervor and strength, which is not particularly helpful.

Obviously, the term *faith* means different things to different people. Much confusion surrounds the term, although most people have a hunch of what one is attempting to describe when the term is used. Clarifying more fully what one is attempting to say can go a long way in making the familiar term most useful by making it more precise.

The clearest and most useful definition of the term is that *faith* is the actual relationship God has established with His people. Faith is that connection we have with the Holy One. It is never a human achievement, but always a gift from God. God bestows this gift upon us insofar as we are open to receive it. In its barest form, *faith is God's pivotal intrusion into our lives.* God kick-starts everything. That is our first inkling that there is even a God. What a startling awakening it is suddenly to become aware that we are here because someone put us here for a specific purpose—that purpose being for God to have someone available to love and care for.

After God's initial self-revelation, the next step in this scenario begins with an invitation from God to have us enter into a meaningful relationship. Attached to this invitation is the activity of God's Holy Spirit who empowers us to respond positively to the Holy One's invitation. Our part in this transaction is our willingness and desire to have this happen. Our role is always one of response rather than initiation.

Imagine being invited by an acquaintance to take a ride in his helicopter. The machine is there ready to take off and the ride is free. All you have to do is say yes, I would like to have this experience. Under those circumstances your willing consent is all that is necessary and you are on your way. You can also say no and refuse the opportunity.

So it is with faith. It begins with God's invitation to us to be in a significant relationship. It is the offer of the gift of *faith*—the offer to live in a loving relationship with the loving Father. The outcome of that invitation is determined only by our willingness to have God become more intimately involved in our lives. Saying "yes, I would like to have this experience" is all that is necessary to be on our way.

How can anyone say no to that? Alas, many people, including profoundly religious individuals, continue to say no or not yet, since I am uncertain about what I might be getting into.

Some people are hesitant to respond positively to God for fear it might change their lives, crimping their style. The truth is, it will change one's life, perhaps radically, but never against one's will, and always for the better. Change will occur! It will prompt increased gratitude for every change God calls into play.

God's involvement in our lives can give birth to amazing *faith*—an unassailable relationship with the Holy One. We can discern Divine involvement in our lives when we sense our spirits leaning into God.

Question

How is the definition of faith as our relationship with God helpful?

Subtle Transformation

The idea of personal transformation strikes different people in different ways. Some people resist change in themselves, and prefer to remain the way they are. They would fear any change that might occur in them could abrogate their existing lifestyle, which they wish to retain. On the other hand, some people may wish they were different in some ways, but are hesitant to trust any outside influence to instigate and carry out any change. Transformation can be both a threat and a promise.

This particular essay casts the occasion of transformation into the realm of authenticating God's involvement in our lives. Any positive transformation occurring in our lives that improves who and how we are indicates that God is most likely involved and active. Self improvement, while desirable, is rare. We seem to need not only motivation to change, but some outside assistance to accomplish it. Some new ingredient is apparently necessary to make significant change in both how we are and what we do. The world of advertisement thrives on promises to change us in ways we desire.

Subtle transformation points to God's involvement in our lives as the chief motivator as well as the major activator who creates any desirable change that we experience.

In considering change in our lives, only narrow mindedness and hard headedness would blind a person from being aware that there is room for improvement in all of us. While we assume we are the highest order in God's creation, we are not at any time all that God created us to be. We are very much a work in progress.

Thus, transformation by divine design is not only appropriate and desirable, it is integral to God's continuous effort to restore us to the originally created state. Transformation is God's never ending offer and effort to make us new creatures, firing on all cylinders rather than missing on some. That is what it means for us to be whole (holy).

Transformation typically happens gradually, although there are examples in history when God had a special mission for someone and increased the voltage to redirect that person instantly and on the spot. In that moment the person was transformed and equipped for the task.

However, for most of us transformation occurs subtly and imperceptibly. We almost need to journal, noting all minor changes in us along the way, then totaling them to get the picture. We would then be able to gauge the total change in retrospect.

There is a depth of joy and gratitude we experience when we do realize that we have become, and still are becoming, better specimens of humanity. We might realize that we are now much less inclined to be critical of another person's weakness or failure. It becomes apparent to us that we are less hostile and slower to seek revenge. Even road rage dissipates. People we dislike lose their grip on our emotions, and we have a surprising inclination to pray for them. We are no longer as arrogant, but quietly content to relate to others in a benevolent manner. We like ourselves much more than before, all the while realizing that what has happened to us is an amazing gift from God. We therefore can rightfully feel assured that God is intimately involved in our lives and is busy transforming us in any number of ways that astound us. Our greatest response is to be filled with gratitude.

There is an old quote from a southern slave when set free that says it well.

> I ain't what I should be.
> I ain't what I wanna be.
> I ain't what I'm gonna be.
> But, thank you, God, I ain't what I usta be.
> —Unknown

It is important for us to have a serious look at ourselves and take inventory.

What aspect of who we are or what we do needs to be changed in order that we become more like we were designed to be? What obstacles or weaknesses need to be overcome in order to make us more whole?

For now we pray that God's transforming power will enter our lives and make us into new creatures, doing new things, or doing old things in new ways, with a more positive attitude. Our perspective of ourselves and of life in general shifts. Something new and wonderful is underway. We are finding life to be far more livable, fulfilling and joyful. If we step out and try it, we will never look back!

Question

How do you feel God has changed your life?

The Urge to Make a Difference

Somewhere inside each of us there is a secret urge to make a difference with our lives. It is a desire to leave our personal handprint on the world—to make it known as far and wide as possible that the world is different because we have been here.

Like many qualities with which God has blessed us, this one also can be corrupted, resulting in horrific travesties. Many world leaders throughout history have usurped power and created havoc for their own people, as well as many other nations, all in an effort to leave their stamp clearly affixed to history. They have wanted their legacy to be one of domination. Their obsession to expand their control has been their response to the urge to make a difference. Alas, their choice of measures pursued has been devastating. The lust for power lies at the bottom of their self assertion.

On the other, more positive, side of this motivating factor is a source of energy that empowers people to do marvelous things. Responding to seemingly hopeless challenges and making a positive difference is more and more prevalent. Benevolence is clear evidence that God is involved. As we find ourselves growing more benevolent along the way, we can be assured that God is truly involved in our lives, shaping us as the potter shapes the clay.

At the outset, our efforts are an understandable response to this urge to make a difference for our own glory. At that juncture it is all about ourselves. Our ego is intricately tied into our actions. It simply feels good to be able to contribute to the well being of others, regardless of our motivation—self centered or benevolent. We have been created with that latent urge, and being able to satisfy it is a remarkable feat.

On a wider plane, the whole matter of making a difference is built into God's creating us. Our mission in life is inherent. We either perceive it, or fail to recognize it and go off on our own, satisfying our egos. Our true mission is singular—find how our God given talents can contribute to the well being of God's people somewhere, somehow. We are specifically called by virtue of our abilities and talents to use them to make a creative and redeeming difference. Every individual has this charge—this sole mission in life. That is our reason for being—to bring pleasure to our Father in Heaven who is overjoyed when we engage in this benevolent behavior.

All of this so far is the response to the universal urge to make a difference. It is a purely natural response. The next level, however, involves a significant transition. The point at which we find ourselves giving God credit for motivating and directing us, something miraculous takes place within us. Grace redeems our urge to make a difference, replacing our former ego driven motive with deeply benevolent concerns. We now see a need and respond to meet it out of gratitude for our own well being. More and more as we find ourselves responding in positive ways out of gratitude and become increasingly aware that God is involved and is changing us. It is God who is moving within us. We sense it; we feel it; it is gratifying and invigorating.

This growing sense of benevolence, and the heightened sensitivity to what is in fact going on inside us, continues to increase. Whether we pursue a career of social service, religion, medicine, education, engineering, business, military or homemaking, the opportunities to serve God's people, maintain peace or preserve God's physical creation open to us ample opportunities to make that difference, and in so doing satisfies that universal urge to leave our handprint as our personal legacy.

The more we allow God to direct us in our thoughts and actions, the better off we and the entire world will be. That is God's modus operandi. His handprint is superimposed over ours.

Question

What would you want as the most important thing to appear in your obituary?

Learning to Live in Two Worlds

Of all the topics in this book, this one is the most exciting to pursue because it leads us into the inner sanctum of our being. While on earth we live in the shadow of heaven which is a momentous gift for which to be grateful beyond measure. Life is good!

Some jokingly say that life is better than the alternative. That notion deserves to be seriously challenged. If we truly live in the shadow of heaven, then that alternative to this life undoubtedly holds considerable promise. It must be something fantastic. The most superlative language we use in describing the most exciting and satisfying things in life is often described as heavenly—the most, the best, the incomparable!

There have been some highly convincing stories reported by people who have experienced what have been labeled as near death experiences (NDE) in which they have described heaven as the most beautiful, colorful, loving and peaceful place that is far beyond anyone's imagination.

If indeed God has chosen to reveal such glimpses into that realm, it only corroborates what has been said and promised by God many times before. While most of us will not experience NDE, we need to be acutely aware of and open to another phenomenon that is not as exclusive as NDE, but fantastic in its own right. It is the incredible option open to us to live mindfully in the spiritual world that swirls within us as well as in the visible physical world that surrounds us.

We are capable of living in two worlds simultaneously because we have been created as spiritual beings as well as physical beings. Our physical nature is most familiar to us. Our spiritual nature is that dimension of our lives that has been created in the image of God who is pure spirit.

We have the option of exercising our spiritual nature, and we are encouraged by God, through countless means, to do so. We can do this through the use of spiritual tools we have been given. Focused quiet time with deep breathing, paying close attention to each breath furnish us with a good starting point. Becoming mindful of our own presence and where we are in the moment is important. Interior, mindful prayer that opens us up to God's presence within us is primary. Allowing God the time and space in our resting minds works wonders in ushering us into that other world of spiritual reality. It is a virtual heavenly experience, and it is now!

Throughout the ages people have sought and received the gifts of spiritual experiences that have taken them into a different world. While this phenomenon is an extraordinary mystical experience, it is not unusual or untypical. Rather, it is a part of the plan for anyone who embarks upon a spiritual journey. Such a journey involves learning to live in both worlds simultaneously—worlds that intersect at many junctures and provide different life experiences, one of which reaches heavenward. It is not at all unusual to discern your connection to heaven while in a prayerful mode. It is a mystical moment and a gift that the Holy Spirit deposits into our lives in quiet and mindful periods.

Some people feel left out because they have not had such experiences. Why they have not is a mystery, as are most things about spirituality. It is not to say that it is impossible for this to happen to anyone. It is to say that God seems to have different gifts for different people. Furthermore, God is full of surprises and who knows what may come your way if you are open to the mysteries of the spiritual world.

Regardless of the nature of the Spirit's gifts, the fact remains we all live in two worlds every day, inevitably, due to our own dual natures and the reality of these two worlds—two kingdoms.

When the thief on the cross asked to be remembered by Jesus when he came into his kingdom, he was saying far more than he understood. In response, Jesus took the concept of the kingdom and defined it with a marvelous response: Today you will be with me in paradise.

As spiritual beings along with our physical nature we are not limited to living within the physical world alone. There is more—far more! The spiritual world—God's kingdom—surrounds us and functions within us. The challenge is to exercise the disciplines of prayer, quiet time and mindfulness that enable us to discern and experience it.

Question

What does it mean to you that you are a spiritual being?

Inspiration—God's Breath of Life

Inspiration is another pivotal function of God's Holy Spirit, and is the initial experience we have that sets us on a spiritual journey. Inspiration initiates our spiritual quest and whets our appetite for more.

While there is a universal yearning for the effects of a spiritually endowed life, one does not simply decide to become spiritual and find success, but is nudged into it by the Holy Spirit who is the prime mover. There is a mysterious flip of the switch which occurs that sets us on our way. When this does occur, it amazes us because it is such an incredible experience. It is like having a new kind of life pumped into us apart from anything we do. It happens, and because it feels so right, so life giving, we are moved to open ourselves to its new perspective, its life changing energy, and its awareness that there is a new and even better way to live. It is palpable evidence of *God's involvement in our lives*.

What we discover is an astounding awareness that life as we have lived it, while considering it quite valuable, is like a partially filled balloon, which now is being inflated. There is a new freshness to life, a stream of joy that washes over us that is invigorating and exciting. At first it comes in brief snatches—glimpses into this new way of being. Then it grows as the inflating balloon.

When we look to see where this comes from, the Holy Spirit appears on the screen. We realize that we are living in the presence of Almighty God who has initiated the entire affair with us.

The original hunger and curiosity that set into motion this new way of living now becomes more urgent, taking on a life of its own. The desire for more and more indicates a healthy appetite for spiritual sustenance. New growth in our inner-most-being spreads into all dimensions of life. Our hearts become softened and more generous. Our love for others flows from a mysterious reservoir deep within. While life does not necessarily become easier, it does become more purposeful, more focused, fueled with a new source of energy. We find ourselves stopping to take a deep breath. Gratitude for everything we are and have becomes a dominate theme in our lives.

As is evident, this new way of living and new way of experiencing God is most desirable. It is the beginning of a new life style—and a newly discovered reason to live.

Very likely, if you have bothered to read this, you have already had some level of spiritual awakening. Congratulations. God has come to you in some fashion that touches you, although it may also puzzle you. You have tasted something new and different.

Now, the imperative at this point is not to try to figure out what is going on—that remains a mystery—but to let the process that God has instigated work its way deeper into your life. Give it freedom to blossom. Let it happen!

Question

How do you feel you have been inspired by God?

The Magic of Silence

Eckhart Tollé has written the delightful book <u>Silence Speaks.</u> While the content is profoundly inspiring, it is the title that holds a powerful secret. Silence speaks! It is magical how silence opens us to greater awareness that God is involved in our lives. There is no message that comes to us from God that is more convincing than those thoughts that God plants in our minds when we put our minds at rest in silence. It is in silence that God speaks to us most convincingly.

The secret to receiving divine messages directly into our minds is learning how to quiet our overactive minds sufficiently, in order to allow God the opportunity to plant God-sourced messages in us. They come to us as thoughts. At first we are convinced we are being creative and indirectly we are. Later we become aware it is God who is the creative one. The Holy One is the greater source and force functioning behind our thinking process, issuing from an endless reservoir of creativity and power. Our function is like a blooming flower. All the elements are present—we just blossom.

As we begin to trust this unlimited resource and act upon its directives, we discover there is validity and excitement in the messages that show up in our minds. If we are willing to listen and trust what God puts into our minds in those moments of silence, these messages amazingly become self validating. We then come to believe somewhere deep inside ourselves that what we are hearing is indeed the mysterious voice of God.

Discernment of the source of these messages is a divine gift, and it comes slowly with experience. At first we sample these thoughts and try them. We become increasingly more skilled at recognizing them and their source.

They are truly efficacious—possessing power within themselves to create trust. They prove their authenticity as we begin to trust them. We walk cautiously at first, but as God's presence accompanies the messages their divine origin becomes increasingly evident.

Our recognition of their divine source does not happen as a mental act or decision, but as an ever growing awareness that things could not be as they are unless it is God who is involved in the process as the instigator—the voice that initiates the process.

Almost always these special messages from God come in moments of silence when we seek to hear and are open to God's voice. Silence can be far more powerful and productive than sound. Of course, we are all different from each other, and God deals with us according to our differences. Yet there is a common reality. Regardless of our various differences, we can all learn to use silence as a powerful tool to move us to receive and trust God's messages that come on our unique wave link.

Silence nourishes our faith as it allows God the opportunity to come to us in a special way. In silence thoughts occur in our minds, and over time convince us of their validity and divine source. In time they prove themselves to be authentic and

worthy of our trust. Our faith is thereby enhanced and enriched.
Silence is magic!

Exercise

Consider setting aside three minutes to practice being silent in God's presence.

Worship—A Hint of Heaven

Worship is a fascinating spiritual phenomenon. It is a necessary ingredient for our total well being as well as an innate urge. We have the propensity to give our devotion to something or someone. We have been created for God's pleasure as well as our own, and worship is a specific part of the pleasure we give to God. In meaningful worship we become vitally engaged with the Holy One, whether the setting is formal or informal, private or corporate.

Our bodies and minds are primarily utilitarian in worship, serving to usher our spirits into the presence of the Holy One. It is important for this scenario to be complete—for the goal of becoming engaged with God to be reached. For this to occur, some disciplining of our bodies and minds is imperative.

For example, preparation for worship, whether in the privacy of our home or in a church setting, is an important first step and one frequently ignored. Disciplining our minds for worship includes quieting our thoughts that race around in our heads doing the Daytona 500. These persistent thoughts need to be reined in and controlled in order for us to focus on our being in the presence of the Holy Father—sincere worship requires intentionality. We should not be cavalier in our approach, but deliberate and determined.

A valuable image of worship is the way it suggests itself to be a *hint of heaven*. Heaven has been described in many ways, including golden streets and pearly gates. These particular images were written in scripture and directed toward the masses of poor and struggling people for whom such images of wealth would hold much attraction. The idea was to make it known that heaven, among many other attributes, is designed to meet every human need we might have.

However we think of heaven as being the ultimate spiritual experience, we need to be clear on one thing.: worship is the penultimate experience of that ultimate heavenly event. The true joy of heaven will not be pearly gates and golden streets, but the intimate engagement with Almighty God, which has been a promise and a puzzle for us for so long.

Everlasting communion with the Holy One and reunion with those we have known and loved during our present earthly stay, will be something that far exceeds anything we can even imagine at this time. Communion in heaven and Holy Communion in worship, are inextricably connected parts of the same phenomenon so let your spirit reach heavenward as you receive those earthly elements of bread and wine.

Furthermore, in heaven there will be peace among all of God's people. How we long for peace in our world now. Worship, in whatever setting, should capture that sense of peace. The exchange of peace in corporate worship hints at ultimate peace. Differences between people should dissolve into gratitude. In our times, worship at its best produces hints of those same heavenly conditions.

Treasures that have been accumulated here and now will

ultimately hold no value, since there will be plenty of everything for everyone. We will all be treated the same. Prejudice will be noticeably missing and greed will be replaced by open generosity. Worship now should reflect and lead us into these heavenly qualities.

It all adds up to a utopian situation, with everything we now know as good, being enhanced to a heightened degree.

Worship centers around God's worth—worth-ship. That is why we sing praises to the Holy One. God is worth our devotion. Nothing we do in worship should take away from that firmly fixed focus on God. The more positive intent we express in our worship, the more it will resemble the heavenly promise.

Additionally, the reading of scripture—God's words to us now—and the elaboration of its meaning in preaching, all point to God's ultimate communication to us. Those words of love, grace, power and promise, all have their roots in worship and their blooming branches in heaven. The connection is much tighter than we often realize.

In those churches where a liturgical form is employed in corporate worship, well chosen thoughts, words and phrases rich with flavorful meaning stand out. These treasured nuggets emphasize particular points that are inspiring because they connect us to the ultimate plan of God's heavenly design.

While life now is filled with work, bills, family, travel, fun and survival at some level, it will all be completed in the heavenly experience. Worship is our opportunity to peek into that ultimate experience and celebrate our participation in God's great plan.

Heaven can never be fully described, only recognized as possessing beauty and love far beyond our imagination. As with many other things pertaining to God, the nature of heaven eludes us and remains a mystery. All worship should emulate that mystery.

Of the many benefits of heaven, the one most significant is that of being with God—living in unending and indescribable love with the Heavenly Father. If heaven, therefore, is living in God's presence, then the true value of worship is in its providing us with a sneak preview of what is to come—being with God in a unique setting.

The church was called into being by God's Holy Spirit on the Day of Pentecost for two purposes. One was to create a community of faith that would recognize and celebrate the fact that however different our religious practices might be, we are all God's people with equal standing. The second purpose is for that gathered community to worship Almighty God in the beauty of holiness.

The value of this community, commonly called the church, is immeasurable. Although it is fraught with massive weaknesses and foibles, its imperfections do not disrupt its mission of providing that essential connecting point between God's people and God. In that respect the church is unique—clearly differentiated from all other benevolent entities. If it is faithful to its true nature and its unique mission of enabling our engagement with God to be realized and enhanced, the church does indeed serve us with heavenly gifts.

Committing ourselves to worship and life within this community can be a wise investment of our time and attention. It pays generous dividends—keeping our focus on ultimate values. A commitment to invest in worship not only will prove to be profitable for enriching our lives—ratcheting up our awareness that God is indeed actively involved with us now—and has even more and better things awaiting us.

Questions

What has been the object of your devotion?
Can you discern God's involvement in it?

Brainstorming with God

Much of this book of essays has been written emphasizing God's constant and persistent involvement in our lives, although we might not be mindful of it at any given moment. This particular piece is being written with a somewhat different slant, although it too speaks of God's involvement with us. The difference is in our pursuit of God's involvement. While God's presence is constant, and divine involvement is ever present, there is a place for our taking action to have God's involvement come into focus and become a leading factor for us.

As we take up the reins, assuming some responsibility in achieving a desired outcome, we move from a passive to an active role. Instead of waiting and watching, we reach out to God and consciously place ourselves in the middle of the action.

This is accomplished by prayerful thought. It is thinking with God—*brainstorming with God*—which can be a most exciting experience. We begin *brainstorming* with a challenge or problem that life has thrust upon us, and we think and ponder how to respond—solve the problem. We invite God into our thinking process to utilize our best thinking in developing a solution. It will therefore become a divinely inspired solution, and we will have been a part of the process. The result will be a timely solution to our problem, plus the thrill of being inspired by the Holy One.

John Baillie, a British theologian, has written many wonderful prayers that are bold and on target. In one prayer he asks God to "suggest my decision." When we intentionally involve ourselves with God—God's having already become involved with us—a connection is completed that serves as a conduit for God's wisdom and creative power mysteriously to enter our minds, enmeshing with our own thoughts, and directing us in solving our immediate problems. This phenomenal process is as functionally reliable as the sun's rising in the east. Although it requires considerable patience, giving time for God to act, it ultimately results in a most convincing and beneficial experience.

The end result of this process is twofold: First, our problem gets solved—God "suggested our decision," although we actually make it. Second, what this does to enhance and enrich our relationship with God is beyond measure. However incredible this experience might seem, there is an amazing high definition of the reality that God has been and still is deeply involved in our lives. Brainstorming with God is stunningly productive.

Question

What decisions with which you have struggled do you feel God has been a guiding influence?

Coffee with God

Relaxing with God over a cup of coffee can be an unbelievably gratifying experience. We do this all the time with our friends. Why not with God, who wants to be our best friend. God wants us to spend time in the Holy Presence, relaxing and soaking up pure glory—having fun.

Scheduling this time together over a cup of coffee, or whatever your favorite drink might be, is a wonderful way to set aside a special time and place to be together. It takes about twenty minutes to drink a cup of coffee. What better way to spend it than with God.

So, pour yourself a cup of java and relax. That takes no serious effort. What comes next does. How to start the conversation? The topic of weather always works: Beautiful day! Good job, God! You give us many gorgeous days. Thanks! We love the sunshine; we need the rain and snow; cloudy days can be relaxing. Today I am planning to . . . (whatever you plan to do); please join me. It would be very special to have you with me all day. Tell me what you have in mind for me today.

Now it is your turn to listen. You must be quiet. Close your eyes. Let your mind wind down. Excuse from your thoughts those extraneous ones that keep storming through. Take a sip and several deep breaths and get ready to listen.

Having dismissed old extraneous thoughts as best as you can, let new thoughts—God-thoughts—enter the sanctuary of your mind.

Now it is time to ask for that treasured gift of discernment that will enable you to recognize God's unique message to you and to differentiate it from all other thoughts you are hosting. It may take more sessions of *coffee with God* for this experience to crystalize into gems of inspiration, but persistence and hope provide the atmosphere for these spiritual gifts to present themselves. Amazingly, when that begins to occur, it is not uncommon to become addicted to this efficacious experience especially if the coffee is good.

Coffee with God is one of the many opportunities open to us for discerning God's involvement in our lives. It can become inexplicably helpful for wading safely through the marshes and quick sands of life. Equally as valuable in this experience is the sheer joy that overarches all of life—the good and the bad—and creates a canopied context of stability and endurance.

Question

Where on a continuum of discomfort to comfort would you place your having a casual conversation with God?

Walking and Talking with God

Spiritual practice enriches our relationship with God. Time spent in prayer and quiet time commits us to God in a highly significant encounter. Time spent talking to and listening to God is what builds that invaluable relationship. It is no different than building relationships with people we want to be our friends. It takes time in each other's presence to make it happen.

While there is similarity between building human friendships and developing a special relationship with God, there is a significant difference as well. With God there is so much more at stake, a fact we often overlook or perhaps choose not to consider. All of life, now and later, is in God's hands, so this relationship is inherently unique. We, therefore, need to pay even closer attention to it than we do in maintaining other relationships.

Unfortunately, it is this special relationship with God that often gets the least amount of our attention and consideration. We allow it to drop to the bottom of our list of concerns. Other relationships, including personal, marital, parental and business connections tend to take precedence over our relationship with God although that should never be the case under any circumstances.

This does not mean those other relationships are unimportant, or we should forsake them. It does mean if we want these temporal human relationships to be of the highest quality, we have the amazing opportunity to undergird them by operating out of our primary relationship with God. This very likely necessitates a critical reordering of things in our lives.

The divine promise is if we seek first the Kingdom of God, these other things will be added. It is a matter of priority. Spending time with God has an incalculable effect upon everything else we do in life. Not only does it keep our directional coordinates in alignment, it engenders within us a clarity of purpose and empowers us to enhance our temporal relationships that fill our days.

It's about *walking and talking with God*. Amazing and incredible things emerge from this resourceful relationship. God speaks to us in unique ways in prayer and quiet time. New ways of living out our days become apparent, making life in general more fulfilling.

This is not an empty promise of religious frivolity, but a bona fide divine commitment that if we spend time *walking and talking with God* all dimensions of our lives become infinitely enriched.

Question

If at sometime you have consciously made an effort to become closer to God what results have you experienced?

Hope—The Sign of God's Activity

The Christian symbol for *hope* is an anchor. The anchor is used to stabilize a ship or boat and hold it in place. The anchor hooks into something below the surface of the water that is stable and strong. That which it hooks into is invisible, but its strength is felt when the line is pulled tight and the anchor holds. We expect the anchor to hold. We expect hope to hold.

So with hope in God. God is our point of connection—invisible but strong, stable and unyielding.

If we are in a boat in a storm, we can be blown off course and perhaps into a troubling and dangerous situation. If we lower an anchor, we may still be tossed about, but not swept into a serious outcome.

Hope is a God-given gift along with the gift of faith. Hope becomes important when we cannot see any resolution to our threatening life situations but continue to hold out there is one. It is the last thing we can cling to when it seems that all else in life has failed us—when there is nothing left that holds any promise for relief, safety or rescue, we have reached the end of all our resources; there is no person, nor any internal strength left to effectuate our survival. It is then we are left with nothing but hope. We have no idea where any help may come from or whether it will ever come at all, yet something within us holds on. That is hope—hope for anything that can help us out of our threatening situation.

Hope is actually an unreasonable expectation something will come to our rescue. Hope is put inside us, and its presence insinuates itself into our lives. It is a phenomenon that escapes our understanding, and is against all odds. It is God's gift—the anchor that holds us steady and secure when life becomes turbulent, unmanageable and threatened.

Hope has another arena in which it operates. It functions inside us whenever we consider our transition into a heavenly existence. While we have no way of knowing what a heavenly state may be like, or whether it even exists, we nevertheless hope. We expect it does exist and we will be included in its reach.

Heaven is invisible to us now, but we feel its pull. We cannot prove it, nor create it, but we hope; we expect there is this continuing phase of God's involvement with us.

One might think, as some do, heaven is all a figment of our imagination—a desperate human construct. Call it what you will, its mere possibility engenders hope and expectation within us. Hints have been dropped; promises have been made. The entire process is evidence that God is involved with us, extending a covenant to us that goes beyond what we experience today in an earthly existence. Our spiritual connection to God, does not end, but transitions into something beyond our present experience and understanding—something that is out of sight, but pulls on us. Thus, we have been given hope and expectation that things presently unseen are yet to come.

Question

How has hope been your saving grace at some time in your life?

Faith versus Fear

Fear has had a tremendous impact on our lives and upon the world. It has been responsible for much ongoing evil throughout history, being the root cause of many wars, creating untold discord and devastation. Former US President, Franklin Delano Roosevelt, once said, "The only thing we have to fear is fear itself." Fear without question is a most destructive and powerful force in all of our lives. Coming to grips with its ominous threat to our well-being is one of life's most important challenges.

There are rare times when fear is appropriate for self defense. However, the extension of fear, beyond what is necessary for survival, totally changes its complexion, making it powerfully destructive. Determining the exact location of that critical transition point between survival and destructive fear is key to a safe and joyful life, versus a severely restricted and burdensome one. The balance is truly vital to our existence and happiness.

When it comes to daily living, we tend to err on the side of destructive fear: fear of failure, fear of loss, fear of loneliness, fear of the unknown, fear of personal inadequacy, fear of being wrong, fear of inadequate resources, fear of growing old, fear of illness, fear of death.

These bountiful fears reduce our lives from what they should be, and can be, severely crippling us and preventing our becoming what God has created us to be. We unwittingly carry this unnecessary burden of fear, thus demeaning our very essence. Our faulty behavior accurately reflects the fear in our lives. Our better judgment is often countermanded by some hidden, but operational, fear we unknowingly entertain. Fear skews our judgment, causing us to make poor choices. It dramatically alters our perception, so we think and act with serious impairment .

Often our criticism of others stems from our own fear of failure or inadequacy. The negativity surrounding most of our fears is ominously debilitating, often causing the very things we fear most to come true.

There is a remedy for a fearful life. It is God's answer—the gift of *faith*—the opposite of *fear*. Faith in this usage is trust in God that gives us confidence and assurance the Holy One's active involvement in our lives will make the difference, enabling us to transcend fear. Our prayer should always be: God empower me to counter my fear with faith that you grant to me.

Faith is one of God's most valuable gifts to us. It puts our living on a completely different level, and orients us in a totally different direction. It frees us from destructive fears that can be so intensely intimidating, and enables us to move forward in life with confidence that God is in charge, and will strengthen us to be equal to any of life's challenges. We need to appropriate the empowering benefits of faith and trust their strength and tenacity.

The great spiritual reality that plays the lead role in all scenarios in our lives is not only that God is with us in all that we do, but does in fact actually live within us, empowering us from the inside to live life confidently and fully. That is the source of our faith—God's indwelling Spirit.

Our prayer should always be that God would grant us this gift of faith that sets us free from those threatening fears consistently seeking to undo us.

While it may be a cliché, the mantra, "Let go and let God," holds for us the ultimate solution to our fear-inclined lives. Letting go is of course the challenge. Fear has such incredible tenacity that letting go of it is no easy move. Yet, it is possible and doable.

It ultimately comes down to that power that dwells within us—God's own Spirit. It is not our strength at work, but that of the Holy One who equips us, enabling us to trust and let ourselves go into the safe arms of God. When we experience that safe haven, the pseudo power of fear is exposed and it loses its grip on us. Faith takes charge and fear evaporates. It takes less than a minute to read this. It may take months even years for it to become a reality for you, so be patient—don't give up. It is not mandatory that you live your life in fear.

While this might sound like begging the question, or be only wishful thinking, the fact is, it works. Let go and let God! Faith neutralizes and exposes the fraudulence of fear. God's love casts out fear. As difficult as it might be to introduce and engage faith and love in our struggle against fear, they are ultimately its only antidote. Be aware that God is always actively engaged with you in this ominous and decisive battle.

Exercise

Consider and describe how fear may have controlled your life at times and how you have handled it.

Experiencing Joy and Pain

Joy is the ultimate positive experience in this earthly segment of life. It is far more profound than happiness and experienced in a totally different way, using very different receptors. Unfortunately, the terms of joy and happiness are frequently used interchangeably, perhaps because the one who confuses them has never experienced true joy. Once one has experienced joy, there is never any confusing it with happiness.

Happiness is a response to circumstances in life, usually in the presence of pleasant events or positives outcomes to one's efforts. Having special people in one's life brings happiness. Life should be filled with an endless stream of good things happening that excite happiness.

On the other hand, joy is a unique state of being which does not switch on and off with changing circumstances. It is a condition of the spirit that remains much more constant and resilient than happiness. Joy is the result of an inward transformation of our whole being that may or may not alter the outward circumstances in which we find ourselves. Joy is a transcendent condition that increasingly occurs as we grow in relationship with God.

It is that faith connection that puts joy into the arena with

God's involvement in our lives. Joy is not a passing emotion, but a highly significant and durable state of being—joyful!

Although durable as an overarching state of being, joy is not necessarily constant. There are dark sides to life that occur with painful regularity. They are the instigators of physical and emotional pain—inevitable and inescapable dimensions of our existence. However, they too can serve a purpose.

Some highly desirable things in life that could potentially bring happiness, seem not meant to be for us, while other things are so threatening and hurtful we can wonder how God allows them to happen. Here we must acknowledge our lack of understanding. We cannot fathom the mind of God! There are no satisfactory, rational answers to that persistent question: why? Rather, we are challenged by painful situations to learn to live within the mystery of God!

We can be certain that these dark and painful experiences do not go unnoticed by God. Whatever their source of origin or whatever their nature, God consistently redeems them, making them into something useful—often a teaching tool. By God's help we grow through pain. In fact, it is quite possible that we grow very little apart from pain—the major edge of our growth being honed by painful experiences.

Growth from pain must not be confused with punishment from God. It is not at all helpful to blame the dark side of life a desire on God's part to punish us. For the most part evil activities or moral failures have an uncanny way of containing within themselves their own inherent punishments. In that sense, we punish ourselves.

God's involvement in life's painful scenarios is not an intent to punish, but ultimately to redeem the situation, converting it into a learning/growing experience. Mysteriously, the very point at which God becomes actively involved, our growth, promoted by our pain, ushers in an overwhelming sense of joy. That becomes the great redeeming transition—*pain into joy!*

The strong connection between joy and pain is not causal, but is nevertheless intricately connected. *Joy* flows out of *pain* when God becomes involved and active, after watching with deep concern as we muddle through. Truly, God is intimately involved in our most intractable situations. Our ability to discern that marvelous and mysterious reality is a true gift, as is all of life from the very outset—pure gift.

Question

The Old Testament seems to express the belief that God punishes with pain-inducing acts. What is your thinking on that idea?

The Heavens Declare the Glory of God

The heavens declare the glory of God,
The firmament shows his handiwork.
Day to day it pours forth speech,
Night to night it declares knowledge.

—Psalm 19:1, 2

Whenever we look up, into what we call the sky, we likely are amazed both by its huge expanse and by its unspeakable beauty. From the earliest time people have been awed by the vastness of what they see above them. The stars and planets have fascinated and charmed people of all ages in all ages. We can observe the *heavens* and be deeply moved by the sheer magnitude of what we see. (See About the Cover, p. 131.)

Those who have studied the astronomical mysteries have discovered definite patterns of movement the heavenly bodies follow, as well as the relationship certain groups have to each other. Although much has been discovered and learned of the heavens, no one would claim to understand fully what all is going on around, above and beyond us. The latest discovery of undulations in the circles around Saturn perhaps caused by two black holes confounds even the most astute astronomical minds.

God has placed us into a setting within this universe and said to us: Although you think the universe is so impressive and mysterious, I want you to know what you see, what I have put together, is merely my hobby. I like to create. Some people have stamp collections. I create and collect stars and planets. I thought you would like my universe so I have shared it. I created it so you might be impressed and thereby drawn to me, and be open to receive other more impressive gifts I wish to give you.

God continues: As with all gifts that anyone gives, the most valuable part of gift-giving is it hopefully enriches the relationship between the giver and recipient—in this case you and me. So as you look into the heavens above you and around you, know what you see is for our joint pleasure. As you behold its wonders, know this is only a reflection of my presence and an inkling of my creative power.

The heavens you see point to my person whom you are invited to know, love and hold in awe. Know there is more behind that heavenly scene. That is only the introduction to what I want you to know and experience.

I have produced what you see in ways that will challenge your best minds to make sense of it. But there is a deeper message behind all of creation. It is the work of my hands to speak in your terms. All of what you see plus much more is my handiwork.

It has been created both for you to enjoy and to attract your attention. Hopefully my work will draw you to me so that I can be your God and you can be my people—my family—my children. I want you to see me as your creator—the one who put you here for my pleasure as well as yours, and for the important purpose of making the world a better place.

Whenever you look up into the heavens, hopefully you will become increasingly aware of my involvement in its existence. As you admire it, and do so with appreciation, know it is all for the ultimate purpose of insinuating my presence into our world—yours and mine. I want you to know in your heart I am inextricably involved in your life. I covet your response and ultimately your awe, praise and worship. I desire above all else that our relationship might be secure and vital.

Question

What emotions do you experience when you look into the sky at night?

Nature—God's Work of Art

God is everywhere, his love is overall
In the sunlight shining, in the trees so tall
. . .
In the rustling grass, I hear him pass.
He speaks to me everywhere.

This wonderful old hymn makes the salient point: God speaks to us everywhere—not in verbal sounds or spoken words—but in signs and signals, shapes and sizes, sunsets and science—*in the sunlight shining, in the trees so tall.* These are messages from the Holy One's creation which paint a picture of God's presence and power. *Nature is God's art work.*

Underlying it all is God's relentless, ongoing miracle of life. That spark of life which ignites the world's endless mass of living things is truly incredible and indicative of God's continuous activity.

Nature is overflowing with insinuations of God's presence and activity. The very way in which the world is put together and functions is a highly convincing message in itself. If we listen carefully, everything about nature will speak to us of the Holy One. If we pay attention, the messages will translate themselves for us. In order to understand these messages and locate their source we must move beyond awe and become discerning.

Alas, many people are prone to turn these gifts of nature into idols, so instead of their being direction-signals pointing us toward God, they are set up as objects of adoration and praise. Rather than being seen as gifts from a majestic and mighty donor who seeks our attention and affection, we mistakenly confuse the gift with the giver—the painting with the artist—nature with God. We connect with the painting, while our perceiving the artist is lost in the shuffle. Nature has become the object of deep affection for countless people, and rightfully so. It is a gift so magnificent and beautiful we are awed by its majesty. However, it must not under any circumstance become the object of our devotion. Admiration and appreciation—yes—devotion—no!

The way to prevent any confusion between the painting and artist is consistently to keep the artist in focus, and acknowledge the awesome beauty of nature by thanking God for the painting each time we behold it. The next time you are struck by some beauty of nature, stop and thank God for the gift. It is right and proper so to do.

The message from God is inherent in nature's beauty and power. Be still—be silent—listen for God's message. With the abundance of spectacular natural scenery surrounding us, we are constantly in a favorable position to receive a plethora of God's endearing messages. It is amazing what we will receive, if we take the time to ponder what is going on, and remain open to whatever God chooses to send our way.

Learning to recognize and interpret God's messages that are

delivered in numerous ways, including via nature, is one of the most satisfying challenges that occurs when we once become aware of what is truly going on—when we get it. The countless things that appear before us, but have previously gone unseen, begin to take shape and assume new meaning. The entire experience is one of having a whole new world open up before us. We are incredulous to realize that all of this has been happening all the time, but until now we have missed the connection between our viewing of nature and God's sending us explicit messages for our direction, comfort, pleasure and spiritual growth.

In the rustling grass, I hear him pass. He speaks to me everywhere.

Question

How difficult is it for you to move beyond the beauty of nature and experience God's presence in it?

Music—Effervescence from God's Soul

There is something ethereal and mystical about music. It touches places inside us nothing else can reach. It has a transforming effect on us. It stirs us—awakening parts of our being that normally lie dormant. Music, with or without lyrics, is one of God's most generous gifts to us—along with our receptacles to receive its energy into our lives..

It is an awakening experience to discern that music, and our ability to appreciate it, are special gifts. Music is unique because its vitalizing messages bubble forth from God's own soul. It is effervescent. When acknowledged for what it is, and from whom it comes, it is unmistakably recognized as a unique gift from God.

Admittedly, not all music is the same. Some nourishes our spirits, while some can have a definite derogatory effect. Music, as well as many of God's gifts, has at times been commandeered and prostituted to serve less than lofty purposes.

That being said, for our exploration into God's involvement in our lives, we want to capture the positive energy of music at its best, because it enhances and enriches our lives. Although different types of music are considered exciting and moving to different people, most music has an inherent power to move the majority of people. Among the many choices with their vast differences, there is always present that common denominator—the power music has to move us deeply.

Whenever we are moved by music, it is then we need to acknowledge it as a gift from God, and give thanks for it as well as our ability to hear and appreciate it. We should never stop with merely receiving this gift, and fail to make the connection with the giver. Regardless of the style or type, if it touches your spirit, it is God's gift to you, so respond to the giver as fully as you respond to the gift. Music is one highly effective way God has created for being involved in your life. It can be a most effective point of connection between you and the Holy One. It is a connection you do not want to miss or ignore.

Furthermore, there is always a message in it for you. Listen for the message as you listen to the music. It will be uniquely directed toward you and will speak to something currently going on in your life. It is uncanny how this works. It may awaken something that has been lying dormant—waiting for this moment. It could meet a specific need; it may suggest a direction in which your life should be moving; it might answer some nagging question with which you have been wrestling; it might produce an aha moment; you may hear something in your mind that has not been present there until now; it could strike a cord you have not previously heard; it could well be new and revealing. Any or all of these promising possibilities may have been waiting in the wings, but they will not become apparent unless you are alert to what is going on. Therefore, pause to apply the template of God's involvement to these potential experiences. Once you do that, the image of God's handprint will begin to emerge—God's message to you will mysteriously take shape within your consciousness.

It doesn't have to be religious music to be from God. All inspiring music has its roots in the divine. However, the religious world has definitely laid claim to a large segment of this enormous musical legacy and developed its own styles.

For the devout person of faith, hymns can be infinitely powerful, and jammed full of invaluable messages to assist in improved living or to comfort the downhearted. Hymns are a mother lode, waiting to be mined. Those hymns that speak to you should be cast into your memory, so you will never be without their treasured resource, even though you might at some point in time lose your faculties of sight and hearing. Hymns contain a particular message, coupled with amazing energy, that nothing else quite duplicates. Claim and develop this rich musical resource. It has the ability to adjust your perspective, redirect and empower your life.

Music speaks to our spirits. Listen—pause—let God speak to you via this unique channel.

Question

What connection have you generally made between your favorite music and your relationship with God?

Making Better Choices

Getting it right is a life long challenge. Whenever we are able to accomplish this feat, something inside us swells up with pride and gratitude. A huge check mark appears beside the notation: well done!

Life is crammed full of choices so more often than not we are bewildered by their countless numbers. Making the correct or even the best choice is a huge victory and deserves celebration.

Unfortunately, we are not always capable of making the right choice. Hopefully, most of our bad choices will have only minimal consequences. We are extremely fortunate whenever our lesser choices do not result in serious long term problems. As we know from experience, this is not always the case, and some of our poorer choices do create serious difficulty for us. That threat, in itself, is a powerful motivator to do our very best to get it right.

An important aspect of living is learning to make the best choices open to us. At the same time we desperately need permission to be imperfect. There is little, if anything, about us that is perfect. Our bodies, minds and spirits are all wounded and scarred with imperfection. We live so much of our lives in spite of our inability to get it right. Yet, the value of getting it right is so great that our efforts to that end are extremely worthwhile. We should never give up the search and struggle.

Many parents encourage their children saying: All we expect of you is to do your best. While that may be adequate support for a learning child, it does not allow for *God's involvement in our lives.* We are not told by God to do the best we can, nor are we left alone to navigate this maze of choices awaiting us daily, even hourly. The good news is we have access to divine guidance in making our choices. We have only to request it.

When we humbly ask God for direction, life's best choices will somehow become more apparent and attainable. While the way this works remains a total mystery, the outcome can be quite astounding. God is concretely trustworthy, and desires the best for us in every situation, desperately wanting to lead us to it. It has been made clear to us, via many modes, it is God's pleasure to be involved with us and guide us through life. This is the most important thought in this essay. Thankfully, we are not left dangling at the mercy of life's major challenges, or even minor ones. We are foolish if we think we must negotiate life's hazardous mine fields using only our own skills. We must constantly remind ourselves we have a divine resource that actually seeks us in our needs, and is pleased beyond measure when called upon to direct and empower us.

We are here to bring pleasure to the Creator who is our divine parent. It brings joy to the Holy One to watch us grow and enjoy the life we have been given. That joy is compounded when our lifestyle becomes one of leaning on God for support and direction in making our decisions.

From our perspective, our joy comes from pleasing God by

making these best choices that simultaneously benefit us, often to our surprise. God's relationship with us is primary, and that alone is the divine purpose that underlies our being here. Pleasing God in return should be a significant motivation for getting it right.

One potent challenge we have in our effort to make the best choice available is the obstinate threat of failure. Regardless of how high or low we set our goals, the lurking presence of failure haunts us. We will fail countless times along the way. It is inevitable. In either thought, word or deed we will miss the mark and come up short. Even with God's assistance we still will not always get it right. This seems too be inherent in our nature.

Although God will certainly forgive our failures, we are still left with the responsibility of dealing with the consequences. Unfortunately, our failures quite frequently affect others, so untangling the snarled results of our poor choices becomes an ongoing, unpleasant chore. However, because we live in a redemptive relationship with the Holy One, we also have divine help with this uncomfortable task.

In these situations, once again, we need to be led by God's direction, which is open ended because of the vastly diverse situations in which we find ourselves. There is no one answer to all questions regarding restitution. However, God will respond and direct us in any serious attempt to make things right, or as right as they can be under any given circumstances.

Throughout this entire process, the difficulty many of us have is recognizing God's direction when it comes. This is a definite lifetime learning process. The first step is to turn it over to God, recognizing that we often are too close to the situation even to see things clearly. Furthermore, we may lack the astuteness to make the best call. So, we must always begin with prayer for guidance, then back away and be patient, giving time for God to recalibrate our perception, thereby enabling us to see things more clearly.

Awaiting divine intervention into our thinking is not easy, and requires a willingness to trust God's system and be patient. Patience is the key to the entire process. Ultimately we still must make the decisions, and we will continue to make mistakes, but we will have been granted divinely inspired thinking to improve our chances and increase our odds for making better choices.

If we take this guidance process seriously, it calls for us to live in close contact with the Holy One. Thus, a prayerful life is required. This includes living every day being oriented toward and open to God. This does not mean we have to focus our attention on God every moment. It does mean we should discipline ourselves to maintain a constant awareness that we live every day in God's sacred presence, and we have continuous access to divine guidance. God is not only present, but persistently present to guide us, while never negating our free will. We must make the decisions, but having sought divine guidance, the best options available are now open to us.

As we gradually learn to trust God's system of guiding our decision-making, we will begin to discern with increasing confidence that God is clearly involved in our lives in highly significant ways—aiding our decision-making being one. If we begin to notice we have been moved to a different track that changes our life's course, and discover that we are indeed making better choices, we should celebrate *God's active involvement in our lives*. What a serendipitous windfall for us!

Question

How do you think God has been involved with you when you have had important decisions to make?

Forgiveness—Healing

There is a strong connection between *forgiveness* and *healing*. It is not a causal relationship in which forgiveness automatically leads to healing, although in some instances it might appear to be that way because of coincidental timing. Instead, the relationship is a parallel one. Forgiveness relates to spiritual phenomena, and healing to physical or emotional phenomena. They are two related and powerful forces God has set into motion, both of which are designed to correct and overcome flaws, mistakes, errors, deficiencies, maladies of all sorts—the bad stuff—sometimes egregious.

God's creation was declared good at the outset. Somehow we, the apex of the created order, have gone astray and taken the rest of creation with us. The creation has been compromised—both its spiritual and physical components. The evidence of this reality is abundant and in our face constantly. Our physical health is constantly being challenged. Likewise, evil abounds and seems to roam freely, persistently challenging us. Not only do we see it all around us, and throughout the world; we also feel it in our own interior (spirit) and exterior (body). It has become quite personal.

These parallel forces of negativity that create illness within our being—body and spirit—are a constant reminder we cannot survive on our own. We desperately need the corrective efforts of God to set things right—to redirect our wandering spirits and heal our ailing bodies.

Remembering the relationship between evil and illness is not causal but parallel—although there can be some crossover—we can observe the healing process that God has established in all of these arenas.

A cut into our flesh sets into motion a corrective healing process that has various stages. One stage of the process is the scabbing over of the wound which is very conspicuous. However, beneath that scab and out of our view, something incredible takes place. The flesh reconstitutes itself and reconnects. It grows back together at its edges—an amazing process to observe.

Parallel to that phenomenon is the healing power of forgiveness, a spiritual rejuvenation. Forgiveness is every bit as incredible as the healing of a physical wound. When God forgives us two things occur.

First, we are set free from the burden of guilt that exists whenever there is a violation and disruption of our relationship with God. Forgiveness leaves us in a state of freedom as if there had never been an offense. Our sin is covered—completely removed from God's sight and concern. In essence it becomes invisible and virtually nonexistent so far as its being disruptive to our relationship with God. We are set free of our guilt. The wondrous truth is we live in a perpetual state of grace and forgiveness.

Second, because our sin and failure wound our spirits, we suffer spiritual injury. The unfortunate effect of this tragedy is that we perceive we have alienated ourselves from God. We fear God is so disappointed with us and may not want anything to do with us. We feel God is no longer present within us, and a certain emptiness pervades our entire being. Our level of discomfort escalates although we might be unaware of the cause of our uneasiness.

Behind the scene and deep within our interior there is always a healing process at work. God is involved and active. There is a spiritual scabbing taking place, and beyond our view an amazing new life is being created. This is the work of God's Holy Spirit, the Great Healer who dwells within us at all times.

The process of these parallel forces of spiritual and physical healing is clear evidence God is involved in our lives. While the evidence is present and seemingly obvious, these parallel phenomena will escape our awareness unless God's own Spirit awakens us and grants us the gift of discernment. By divine grace we can receive this holy gift of discernment and reap the benefits of forgiveness and healing. The experience of profound joy comes with these blessed phenomena.

There is a flip side to guilt and forgiveness that the Lord's Prayer sets forth. It is forgiving those who have offended us. Forgiving those who offend us is as important as our being forgiven. Holding a grudge or being unable to forgive is a heavy burden to carry, and the burden is always ours, the offended. If we continue refusing to forgive our offender, or find it impossible, the weight we are sentenced to carry can be extremely debilitating.

It is patently true it can be very difficult to forgive others—sometimes it is beyond our ability to do so. However, we are always invited to ask God for the ability to do it. God will certainly bestow on us this much needed gift. It is a precious gift to be able to forgive, and it brings healing to us.

It is helpful to begin this process by praying for our offender. In this process something inside us miraculously changes. We begin to see our offender in a different light—as a child of God as surely as we are.

Whenever we find ourselves forgiving others, it is a wow moment. In those moments we should become aware God is actively involved in our lives, enabling us to let go of the burden which otherwise could become cancerous to us.

One of the most difficult situations in which forgiveness seems almost impossible to employ is in cases of sexual abuse, especially when it is carried out by some family member. These devastating injuries require an incalculable amount of God's healing grace.

Even in a family that harbors such evil members, God becomes deeply involved in an amazing, redemptive process, distilling the lives of victimized people into something extraordinary—even magnanimous. Many outstanding people, renowned for their benevolent actions, have come out of the most abusive home environments. It seems as though God, ever so tenderly, reaches in and lifts out these special people who are seen as being uniquely suited for special missions. These victims are equipped to perform unbelievable acts of mercy and kindness, not in spite of their horrific experiences, but because of them. The way that energy gets transformed, from negative to positive, is an amazing act of God.

As stated, evil abounds in the world, and ensnares people who become horrendously destructive. Still God edges into the lives of those people who are victims of such evil acts, and anoints them, if they so allow. By God's abundant grace they become saints in their own right. Their very struggle gives them greater strength, and their ministry can be transformed into deep caring, because of their own trauma and healing.

Fitness trainers tell us that strenuous exercise tears muscles which when healed become stronger than before. The scar tissues add strength. That can also be true for the torn hearts of people who have been victimized by evil perpetrators. The scar tissues that develop from torn and healing hearts can make them into strong but tender-hearted saints. This amazing transformation can prime them to care for others in ways untested, uninjured persons cannot. Hearts torn asunder then healed by God's grace are groomed to make huge contributions that heal, enhance and nourish the people around them.

As Jesus was victimized by Judas' betrayal, our Heavenly Father transformed the results of that very evil deed into an act of redeeming love and grace—crucifixion and resurrection. Similar transformation can occur in those persons whose lives have been devastated by the evil deeds of a perpetrator.

It is beyond our understanding how God works this redemptive process to heal and turn things around so dramatically. However, there is ample evidence that this is going on all the time because God is persistently and actively involved.

Questions

How fully have you experienced God's forgiveness? Partially? Fully?

How has feeling forgiven changed your ability to forgive others?

Healing of the Mind

It seems as though the healing of the mind has not received the degree of concern and attention the healing of the body has. There is an entire army of medical providers who are committed to healing the body. The size of the cadre of forces dedicated to healing the mind is certainly noteworthy, but remains quite a bit smaller than the medical corps dedicated to physical healing.

While considerable progress has been made in the fields of psychiatry, psychology and counseling, the intricacies of the mind nevertheless remain elusive. We do know the function of the mind is tied to the brain, which is part of our physical anatomy, but the nature of that function is only minimally understood.

Unfortunately, there are among us, people whose minds are quite ill. Horrific atrocities are the products of these distorted minds. Wars have been fought; massacres and suicide bombings have occurred; the high incidence of individual suicides are all incomprehensible acts emanating from sick, troubled minds. The debilitating effects of mental illness have created havoc in countless interpersonal relationships that otherwise might be happy and healthy.

Thankfully, modern medicine, along with skilled therapy have helped to suppress a significant number of these mental disturbances, as well as reduce the severity of their impact. However, the situation remains serious.

So, where does God come onto the scene? How and where does God's involvement show up? For whatever reason the divine presence seems to be less apparent in these situations than in physical healing. In the cases where healing of the mind does occur, it seems the process is frustratingly subtle.

Because of its subtlety it is easy to overlook *God's involvement* in the medical dimension of this phenomenon. Medical practice is such a highly esteemed institution in our culture it seems to stand alone and apart from God's involvement. However, in spite of its distinguished position, it does not stand alone, but is very much a tool which God employs for human benefit. God's handprint is all over medical knowledge and procedures. Medical personnel have been endowed with bright and open minds which are God's gifts to them, and us. They have been divinely led into the arena where healing of sick minds does occur.

Likewise, psychologists and counselors, along with their medical compatriots, do not appear on the scene by happenstance. Although it is not often acknowledged, they have definitely been called and led into these healing professions by virtue of their God given talents and concerns—all of which are awakened within them by God's Holy Spirit.

God's use of human resources in any activity does not make it any less a divine activity. In the healing of the mind, as in countless other life situations, God's involvement is discernible to the open and searching person. It is more evident in some cases than in others, but the faithful spirit learns to perceive this divine involvement and respond in profound gratitude. Thanks be to God!

Question

What is your thinking on how God uses the medical world to bring healing to us?

God's Uncanny Timing

While some of God's involvement in our lives can be difficult to discern, one that is so obvious, even blatant, is the uncanny and timely appearance of a person or persons in our lives, who are just what we need at that time. God directs a highly sophisticated system of personnel logistics and timing. Following the trail of God's uncanny activity can become unduly challenging but highly inspiring.

For example: a person whose training and/or experience is the very thing needed at a given moment somehow shows up and comes to our aid; a caregiver is desperately needed to assist in the care of an aging parent—a name is casually mentioned—when pursued it is discovered that the person has just left another job and is available immediately at an affordable rate; a person is riding in the passenger seat of his car—not driving—in the immediate proximity of a hospital when a seizure occurs. Another seizure occurs in the emergency room. Medical testing reveals a brain tumor, shortly thereafter removed successfully. Coincidence? Not for the believing heart. A job opportunity opens up and appears to be an exact fit. Because it is so ideal there are many applicants. While one might be qualified, so are many others. Someone else has been chosen. The job is lost.

Then comes a call. Something strange has occurred. The candidate offered the job has taken another job. The opening is back on the table. The job is yours. The luck of the draw—or God's activity? The person of faith recognizes and acknowledges divine activity.

However difficult it may be even to consider that God could possibly focus on our individual needs, it is easy for a person of faith to recognize and acknowledge God's involvement whenever this occurs, as it so often does.

This strategic and timely placement of persons in our lives extends beyond emergency situations. It is a common occurrence. Look at your family. Most of us have come into our families by the most natural process of being born into them. Many of us have been extremely blessed by having loving and benevolent parents. If one is so blessed, it should be automatic to give credit to God for this most gracious gift.

God also watches over us and keeps us safe. While there are endless accidents and misfortunes throughout life, there are also countless times when these incidents have been averted and avoided to our amazement. Why and how did we get spared? How many times have we narrowly missed being in an automobile accident without being aware of its threat, until after the fact? We did nothing to save ourselves because we were not even aware of the danger, but in retrospect we should have been involved—but were not. The believing heart gives thanks to God for intervening. The timing had been uncanny.

A difference in perception is obvious. Some would say that sheer luck was at play. Others, who seek to discern God's active involvement in their lives would award the credit to the Holy One. Either we believe God is involved in our lives or we don't. If we do so believe, then there is no limit to where this can take us, although we must use discretion in awarding credit. Through experience we learn to live on that high plane of a divinely inspired life. We aptly acknowledge how life is so different when we learn to live it with the constant awareness of God's involvement—the gift of the indwelling Spirit. It then becomes quite natural for us to attribute these uncanny events of timing to the Holy One.

Question

What experiences have you had that you would attribute to God's uncanny activity?

Transcending Excessive Stress

Of all the issues and subjects written about in these essays, this particular one concerning *stress* is perhaps the most timely one, because of the demanding nature of our kaleidoscopic culture.

At the outset, it needs to be clearly established that if God is truly involved in our lives, then there is always a divine presence with us, including those times when we find ourselves in excessively stressful situations. Whenever this occurs it is extremely important for us to stop in our tracks and take inventory of those things either we or surrounding circumstances have put on our plate. It is much wiser to recognize and confront these issues early on, rather than allowing them time to gain momentum and secure the advantage over us, creating undue stress.

What is the scene; what are we involved in; what have we allowed to claim our attention; what consumes our energy; what defines our daily schedule; which of our relationships enhance our well being, and which ones are stressful and unhealthy? Do we monitor and control which issues we allow to occupy our thoughts and engage our emotions? Countless numbers of issues hold the potential for creating excessive stress in our lives.

Stress can be lethal at its worst, and severely debilitating at the very least. It is one of the most damaging forces in our lives along with fear. Unfortunately, our culture thrives on stressful situations. Being stressed is the new normal. Consequently, our physical and mental health are in serious jeopardy. We must find a way to neutralize stress and navigate life more efficiently.

Parenthetically, it should be made clear not all stress is inherently destructive. A certain amount is essential for survival. Simple movements that are required to live, even random thoughts create minimal stress. Stress serves us well when we must make a fight or flight decision. However, moderate stress is not the norm for us in our society today. Excessive stress is the new norm. How should we handle this negative impulse?

Developing a highly functioning spiritual orientation to life is certainly one of the best antidotes to this destructive power, because it enables us to transcend excessive stress. It lifts us out of the reach of its powerful tentacles used to ensnare and overpower us.

How does a highly functioning spiritual life enable us to remain healthy in a stress producing culture? It sensitizes our ability to hear the depths and grasp the truth of God's message to us. It empowers us to act upon this invitation and promise: "Come to me when you are heavily laden and I will give you rest." Matthew 11:28

The authentic and empowering message from God is the Holy One is deeply and intimately involved with us. This divine power can become our power, to deal with whatever situations threaten us. Imagine having access to this kind of power! If we are wise enough to adopt this power we can be mysteriously raised above the fray. Mystery is an especially important element in this instance because the solution, like the problem, escapes our comprehension. It is truly a mystery!

In the midst of any upsetting upheaval we can be given the gracious gift of peace—a peace that passes all understanding. We are reminded with considerable emphasis the issues that threaten to undo us are but child's play for God. We become aware the excessive stress which threatens us is in essence a scam designed to demobilize us. If left unchallenged the stress will inevitably consume us. However, if God takes over, the scam is exposed, and we escape the threatened devastation.

The Biblical statement, "Cast all your cares on him, he cares for you (I Peter 5:7)," is a clear invitation to shift the burden of our stress to God who handles things far better than we can. This is a critical shift that holds the promise to unburden us. Making this shift requires we learn how to make it happen. Herein lies the key!

This is a mental exercise using spiritual energy. It is brought about by prayerful thought that God can and will lift us above the threatening situation into a place of peace. From this advantageous position we are given the perception we are now out of reach of the tentacles of stress that initially ensnared us. Ironically, we might still be in the very same situation, having to cope, but a miraculous change has occurred in the way we now envision it, and in turn experience it. We are free to cope with it in an unstressed manner. We continue to do the work, but God now carries the burden of stress. What a mountainous burden is lifted! It is gone. The relief is indescribable.

The way for us to remove ourselves emotionally from the arena of stress is to let go and let God. This is an amazing mantra to remember and use, and is the most helpful tool we have at our disposal for dealing with life's trying challenges.

This transferring of the underlying cause of stress to the God department for resolution is easy to describe, but quite challenging to act upon and bring about. However, if we are persistent and patient it can be done under God's guidance. There is no better method to control excessive stress in our lives.

It is helpful when praying for relief from stress and attempting to turn over to God the culprit cause of stress, we not ask for specific changes, but let God determine how to change the stifling scene. If we try to direct God to make specific changes of our choice and God chooses a more effective alternative, we might not recognize the change as coming from God. So let go and let God!

Only then are we removed from the fray. We might still be involved in the situation, but it is God who now gives impetus to the resolution because we have turned everything over to the Heavenly Father. Down the line, in retrospect, we will be able to recognize God's handprint on the solution. We can then discern God has once again demonstrated divine involvement in our lives.

The Serenity Prayer is a powerful resource when we find ourselves in a situation that would ordinarily stress us: "God, grant me the serenity to accept the things I cannot change, the courage to change the things I can, and the wisdom to know the difference." Serenity—courage—wisdom. God can and will grant these special tools we need to deal with circumstances into which life casts us, and to which we commonly respond by becoming unduly stressed.

It is not inevitable that we succumb to the damaging effects of stress. Two steps, if taken, can help offset the damage. First, pray, asking God not only to take the pressure off you, then let go. Before moving on, take a deep breath, then blow it out, releasing the pressure. Second, ask God not only to take the pressure off, but actually to create and reveal a solution to the existing problem and acknowledge that such a solution at this point is probably off your radar.

This process of turning things over to God to resolve can become your new modes operandi if you trust God to be active in your life. It all begins with hope—expectation things will improve. Gradually hope morphs into trust—trust in God will take charge. That is when the burden begins to shift. For this apparent miracle to happen, allowing us to transcend stress, it must be pursued with hope, commitment and trust.

Every time we experience this process of transcending excessive stress, we rise to another level of living. From that much more comfortable stance we might well look back wondering why we have been so slow learning the tremendous difference it makes when God is engaged and given the freedom to function. Because stress is so common and devastatingly destructive, it is imperative we deal with it and not let it control our lives. The most promising way of doing this is to appropriate God's willing and eager assistance. Let go and let God!

Question

What more would you want from God to help you deal with excessive stress?

Transcending Temptation

Temptation is a slippery slope. The first step often is the end of our ability to control ourselves. Thankfully, forgiveness hangs around to retrieve us at the bottom of the slope. Experiencing the power of forgiveness can also strengthen us to resist taking that first step the next time. Forgiveness is one of God's immeasurable gifts. It never fails to rescue us whenever the need arises.

The most amazing thing for people of faith is that we always live within a state of forgiveness. Forgiveness actually precedes our wrongful thoughts, words or deeds, because God has already created the gift of forgiveness and the mechanism for dispensing it, once and for all. That is what Jesus came to effectuate. Forgiveness is perpetually in force.

Having put forgiveness into perspective, the matter of dealing with temptation, with all of its poisonous tentacles, needs to be brought front and center. Forgiveness heals, but unfortunately scars remain and often the pain continues. Preemptively confronting and somehow overcoming temptation is God's first choice for us.

Averting temptation or dealing with it from a position of strength, rather than succumbing to its power, is certainly the better way to go. In doing so we must first be cognizant we will forever be threatened by its omnipresence. We are always wishing to dismiss it with a wink, not fully convinced we do not secretly want to wade in and enjoy the promised thrill of sliding down the slippery slope.

Parenthetically, we need to be aware some of our most troublesome and pernicious temptations have to do with omission—failing to act when or as fully as we should. For example, we are often in a position to alleviate the pain or suffering of someone, but feel unduly put upon if we reach out to help. The subtlety of such temptations makes them deceptive. It is easy to rationalize our way out of providing assistance that would make a huge difference in someone's life. Since these types of temptations are perhaps our greatest downfall, they too must be included among serious threats to us.

The reason temptation is such a menace is because of our own nature. We are not Holy (whole) as God is Holy. Our nature is tainted and warped. We seem to be inclined toward evil and certainly attracted to it. We cannot change that universal reality. While we can and do carry out many good deeds, we are nevertheless burdened with this inclination toward evil. It will never cease to hold some hidden appeal to us. We can slip into it, be fooled by it, host it in our personalities and forever be haunted by its presence in our innermost being. It is truly a scourge.

If God would leave us to ourselves we would surely self destruct. We are constantly in a struggle with temptation that presents itself to us in the multiform of thought and word as well as deed. Against those odds we scarcely stand a chance—if we try to withstand it alone.

Having painted the sad picture of our human predicament, we are not to despair. Help is on the way. What we cannot do ourselves can be done for us and through us by the Holy One who comes to our aid and rescue.

While we are all but helpless to deal alone with our flawed nature in the face of temptation, we are promised assistance to deal with the problem. God the Father has sent the Holy Spirit to intervene in this struggle—to give us outside help enabling us to function from a position of strength and hope, rather than from our own innate and inept weakness. This divine strength transcends our own strength, empowers us to hold fast, transcend temptation and not take that step onto the slippery slope.

The battle is fierce and the consequences can be horribly frightening. Failure looms, and all too often scores. We have been there before. At least we are clear that it is wrong to take that first step. We have been given an awareness. The stakes are much higher than we can even imagine. While we might well survive surrendering to any single temptation, there is always the accumulative effect—the slippery slope.

The stage is frequently set with a scene of frivolous promise of personal gain, pleasure, success or an outlet for our anger and frustration. We are promised an outcome that cannot occur. Temptation is always a scam. We are reminded of Jesus' temptation. It was a lie! Temptation is a totally dishonest sales pitch having no credibility.

Thankfully, we have inside us an alarm system that warns us all this is not true. That awareness inside us comes from our consciouses God's Spirit has sharpened. It alerts us to the pending danger. It is that still small voice within.

This awareness of the hovering threat, and the falseness of its promise, may not be enough to scare us away from the enchantment of the temptation or the urge to act upon it. It merely alerts us to the dangers that are facing us. It grudgingly presents us with an alternative choice and another resource for resisting the power of the temptation.

Whenever we find ourselves in such a situation and feel helplessly unable to cope, we are promised God's power which is the only power that can enable us to resist. This source of strength to resist is readily available to us and comes to us for the asking. Once again prayer solves many problems, and when dealing with temptation very likely is the most useful and effective tool available to us.

Whenever temptation comes our way, it is incumbent upon us to listen to that alert system God has installed within us. Listen for God's message. Then it is time to ask for help in order to avoid the consequences of sliding down that slippery slope. Whenever God says *no* we can hear the message in our conscience. The sound resonates within us. We recognize that voice. That moment is critical and its outcome will make a huge difference. Our response is pivotal. What do we do?

At our invitation to come to our aid and intervene, God shows up on the scene with an entire arsenal, plus a bag of tricks we can use to counter the threat we experience.

In this bag of tricks there are some clear-cut ways of exiting from the moment of temptation with success. The most successful one, for example, is to pause and pray for the people whose presence or behavior create in us feelings of anger, hate, lust or desire to seek revenge. Although it is difficult at first, pray earnestly for the people who are obnoxious, nosey, aggressive or militant. It dissipates the urge we experience to think, say or do something negative that would escalate the tension.

It is also quite helpful to remember the trigger person is a child of God whom God loves deeply. The ultimate secret: pray that God will grant a special blessing to that person. It is amazing how effective this deflective tool can be if used with sincerity. As is true with all tools, learning to use them is awkward at first, but we can become more efficient with practice.

Transcending temptation ultimately comes down to our appropriating and utilizing God's intervening power as the pivotal ingredient at the critical moment. If and when we are successful, it becomes obvious that *God is actively involved in our lives.*

Suggested prayer when faced with temptation: I need your help, Holy One, to resist this temptation that is now in my face. Especially bless the person(s) who might have triggered this temptation. You have alerted me to its danger. Please deliver me from evil. Lift me above it, so that its power over me is neutralized and negated. Stay with me and empower me to stay with you. Only with you am I safe.

Question

What temptations has God helped you resist or transcend?

Struggling with Depression

There is an ancient Chinese affirmation used in QiGong that has interesting spiritual overtones. ". . . I am filled with peace and joy; I am free of pain and illness; I am blessed with good fortune." This is a statement that can relate to the common condition of *depression*.

Depression appears to occur in two forms and to have two separate and distinct causes. First, there is the clinical form. Second, there is the situational form.

Both forms are serious and debilitating. Each must be treated in a particular way different from the other.

In the case of the clinical form God uses and directs the knowledge and resources which the medical world has developed to bring the healing of this onerous condition. In the case of situational depression, created by downturns in life, God's active involvement can bring direct healing. This magnanimous blessing remains in perpetual readiness for tapping, but sadly is frequently left lying idly on the table.

Life is full of pot holes, downturns and sheer bad luck. Many of life's negative experiences go far beyond ordinary challenges, becoming uncontrollably destructive, defeating and depressing.

The religious world has historically used intercessory prayer on behalf of people struggling in depressing situations. The major thrust of this prayerful function is to have God alter the burdensome situation that is causing the depression, if possible, thereby opening the way for healing to occur. It is a sort of divine surgery—remove the malignancy—so healing can take place.

Another dimension of this condition of situational depression has to do with learning to live within the challenging situation. With God's help, develop an accepting attitude regarding what is happening that may not be changeable.

Coming to grips with situational depression can be a full blown spiritual experience requiring a God-induced perceptual shift. Changing our perception of a situation can be a tremendous challenge even though it does offer great relief.

There is a fascinating discipline called Phenomenology that deals with perception. The core teaching of this discipline is things are not necessarily as they appear to be. The classical example—pictures depicting stairs creating an illusion. At first, it appears that the stairs go in one direction—as you continue looking at the illustration, your perception of the stairs suddenly switches and the stairs appear to be going in the exact opposite direction. Which way are the stairs really going? Conclusion: the direction depends upon one's perception. The message: perceptions vary and therefore are not always reliable or accurate. They can be skewed, and they change. Situational depression frequently occurs because of faulty perception. We see things as being one way, while in fact they are not that way at all.

The same is true of attitudes. Attitudes are fixed conclusions at which we have arrived resulting from our perceptions. Attitudes are our orientation to life and determine how we live. Because our attitudes are tied to our perceptions, they too can be equally off-base and ill informed. They might need to be changed in order to relieve the pressure of depression. Changing our attitudes is truly a rigorous endeavor—a spiritual experience in which God's power must necessarily be engaged.

Our perceptions and concomitant attitudes change as we alter our mental focus from a particularly negative orientation, to *God's active involvement in our lives.* If and when we shift our thoughts to the reality of God's power at work in our lives, the corrosive effect of depression begins to lose its power over us. When we redirect our focus from the immediate negative situation to the larger picture of God's being in charge, and fulfilling the divine promise to lift us out of the reach of the threatening grasp of depression, then healing can become a reality.

Situational depression is not an innocuous force, but a very strong and debilitating one. Furthermore, it is not something we can change for ourselves, but requires divine intervention. However, when divine intervention does work its wonders, we are surprised by relief.

The well known Serenity Prayer, mentioned in an earlier essay, but worth repeating here, can be extremely helpful in many depressing situations. "God grant me the serenity to accept the things I cannot change, the courage to change the things I can, and the wisdom to know the difference."

Prayerful surrender to God's direction and healing power is a tremendous blessing. It has the capacity of enabling us to overcome situational depression by changing our perspective, and in turn our attitude, which in turn changes our entire orientation to life. As grace-filled as that gift can be, it must not be confused with God's other gift of medical assistance, when that is the appropriate approach to clinical depression. In many situations both medical and spiritual approaches used in tandem can be effective.

God is involved with us in all healing. Whenever healing does occur we would do well to note the divine handprint and give thanks.

Questions

In what depressing situations have you asked for God's help? How helpful was it to bring God in on the cause?

Conclusion

After having read this material, you may have an array of responses and feelings. If you have been inspired, you are probably grateful and ready to move on with increased enthusiasm.

If you are questioning the validity of the material, there is a simple way either to authenticate it or, on the other hand, find reason to dismiss it. Before you either commit to its credibility or readily dismiss it, you owe it to yourself to risk trusting it at least enough to test it.

When ice fishing, safety is of primary concern, so it is prudent to check the thickness of the ice as you move out onto it. If it is not obvious how thick it is, you drill holes through it near the shore, so if you fall through it is not life threatening. If it proves to be safely thick, you move out a little deeper checking it as you proceed. You continue to move out as it proves to be thick enough to support you, or else you get off, if it doesn't. Whether or not you continue depends upon the reliability of the ice.

This same strategy can be used to check the validity of the material in these essays, as it relates to you. For example, see how far God's answers to your prayers allow you to continue your movement forward and become more deeply involved.

Historically, these thoughts and ideas have proved to be solid and totally safe to trust. History is replete with persons who have committed to living their lives in such a spiritual lifestyle.

Not every professing Christian desires or is willing to trust the reliability of God's involvement in their lives. However, those who do inevitably will discover a whole new way of life—a life filled with hope, joy and eager expectation. All of life begins to make much more sense as we become increasingly aware of why we are here in the first place. Life may be bewildering until we are awakened to the truth that our relationship with God is our raison d'être.

All of the topics presented herein are interconnected at some level. However, you may find some topics more enlightening and meaningful, while others remain puzzling. If that represents your experience, then set aside those that make you feel uncomfortable. You can come back to them later, if you desire or are so led.

Conversely, pursue with abandonment those topics you feel are uncannily written explicitly for you. They are the ones that meet your need at the moment, so spend time with them. Reread them again and again. Let them energize you, answer your long held questions, resolve your most serious reservations, awaken your spirit from dormancy, move you to a more prayerful lifestyle, strike a note of pleasant harmony within you, or any other positive response you might feel.

Most importantly, if there is anything that especially resonates within you, hold on to it and let it incubate—percolate. God has unpredictable ways of reaching us, some quite miraculous. Be open to whatever God sends your way.

So, stop, be still! Quiet your mind. Breathe deeply—again—and again. There is a reason why breath and spirit are the same word in Greek, the language of the New Testament. Consciously breathing deeply while being mindful of the moment can be a profoundly spiritual act.

Give thanks! A grateful heart is open to both God and the world. Let your newly emerging lifestyle lead you boldly into every new today—after all, today is all we ever have. Be patient!

Live anchored to our Heavenly Father with high expectations and open to surprises.

About the Cover

The cover has been designed by Steve Hays of Steve Hays & Associates Graphic Design.

The background photography for both the front and back cover was taken in Australia by Greg Halac, whose fascinating description follows.

The Milky Way's rising image focuses on the star-rich part of our galaxy best viewed from southern latitudes. The center of our Milky Way Galaxy is 1/4 of the way along the image diagonal from the lower left corner. We are ~25,000 light years from the galaxy center (1 light-year is how long light travels in 1 year, ~6 trillion miles). The Milky Way has an estimated 200 billion stars in it, and is ~120,000 light years in diameter. Our galaxy is 1 of ~100 billion estimated to exist in our visible universe.